MathFlare

Name: ____________________

Class: __________

Teacher: ____________________

Introduction

As parents and educators, we recognize the pivotal role mathematics plays in shaping a child's academic journey and future success. Yet, the path to mathematical proficiency can often seem daunting, fraught with challenges and complexities. That's where the transformative power of MathFlare Workbooks shine through, illuminating the way forward with clarity, precision, and purpose.

Introducing MathFlare Workbooks – a beacon of guidance, a testament to excellence, and a catalyst for achievement. Crafted with meticulous care and expertise, MathFlare Workbooks stand as paragons of educational excellence, designed to nurture young minds, ignite a passion for learning, and develop a deep-rooted understanding of mathematical concepts.

Picture this: your child eagerly delves into the pages of Mathflare Workbook, greeted by a step-by-step guide illuminated with vivid examples that demystify complex mathematical concepts. With each turn of the page, they embark on a journey of discovery, encountering thoughtfully curated practice questions that reinforce learning and hone problem-solving skills. And when they unveil the answers to those very questions, a sense of accomplishment blossoms within them – a tangible reward for their hard work and dedication.

But MathFlare Workbooks are more than just tools for learning; they are pathways to comprehension, fostering a deep-seated understanding of mathematical concepts through a sequential, logical flow. From fundamental principles to advanced problem-solving strategies, every chapter builds upon the last, ensuring a robust foundation upon which future knowledge can be constructed.

As parents, we yearn for nothing more than to see our children thrive, to witness the spark of inspiration ignited within them as they conquer academic challenges with confidence and poise. MathFlare Workbooks serve as partners in this noble endeavor, offering not just practice questions, but the keys to unlocking a world of opportunity.

And for teachers, MathFlare Workbooks stand as invaluable allies in the quest to cultivate mathematical proficiency in the classroom. With answers readily available, instructors can focus on guiding and nurturing their students, confident in the knowledge that MathFlare Workbooks provide a solid framework upon which to build.

In the pages of MathFlare Workbooks, we find not just the promise of academic excellence, but the seeds of a brighter tomorrow. So let us embrace the power of mathematics, let us champion the journey of learning, and let us pave the way for a generation of young minds poised to shape the world. With MathFlare Workbooks as our guide, the possibilities are infinite, and the future, bright.

Table of Contents

Algebra 1	
Order of Operations (PEMDAS)	1
Solving Two-Step Equations	8
Solving Multi-Step Equations	16
Equations Two-Side	23
Simplify Expressions	30
Evaluating Equations	43
Standard Linear Equations	53
Quadratic Equations	56

MathFlare
MATH WORKBOOK
Grade 2
Step by Step Guide and Essential Practice with Answers
Addition Subtraction
Multiplication
Place Value and Expanded Notations
Geometry
MathFlare Publishing

MathFlare
MATH WORKBOOK
Grade 2-3
Step by Step Guide and Essential Practice with Answers
Addition Subtraction
Multiplication and Division
Place Value and Expanded Notations
Geometry
MathFlare Publishing

MathFlare
MATH WORKBOOK
Grade 3
Step by Step Guide and Essential Practice with Answers
Multiplication and Division
Decimals
Place Value and Expanded Notations
Fractions and Geometry
MathFlare Publishing

MathFlare
MATH WORKBOOK
Grade 1
Step by Step Guide and Essential Practice with Answers
Counting and Numbers
Addition and Subtraction
Place Value and Expanded Notations
Understanding Time
MathFlare Publishing

MathFlare
MATH WORKBOOK
Grade 1-2
Step by Step Guide and Essential Practice with Answers
Counting and Numbers
Addition and Subtraction
Place Value and Expanded Notations
Understanding Time
MathFlare Publishing

MathFlare
MATH WORKBOOK
Grade 3-4
Step by Step Guide and Essential Practice with Answers
Addition Subtraction
Multiplication Division
Place Value and Expanded Notations
Fractions and Geometry
MathFlare Publishing

MathFlare
MATH WORKBOOK
Grade 4
Step by Step Guide and Essential Practice with Answers
Addition Subtraction
Multiplication Division
Place Value and Expanded Notations
Fractions and Geometry
MathFlare Publishing

MathFlare
MATH WORKBOOK
Grade 4-5
Step by Step Guide and Essential Practice with Answers
Multiplication Division
Place Value and Expanded Notations
Fractions and Geometry
Unit Conversion
MathFlare Publishing

MathFlare
Grade 5
MATH WORKBOOK
Multiplication Division
Place Value and Expanded Notations
Fractions and Geometry
Unit Conversion
Step by Step Guide and Essential Practice with Answers
MathFlare Publishing

MathFlare
Grade 5-6
MATH WORKBOOK
Multiplication Division
Place Value and Expanded Notations
Fractions and Geometry
Units and Statistics
Step by Step Guide and Essential Practice with Answers
MathFlare Publishing

MathFlare
Grade 6
MATH WORKBOOK
Integers and Statistics
Arithmetic and Pre-Algebra
Fractions and Geometry
Ratio and Percentage
Step by Step Guide and Essential Practice with Answers
MathFlare Publishing

MathFlare
Grade 6-7
MATH WORKBOOK
Arithmetic and Pre-Algebra
Ratio, Percent Proportion
Geometry
Statistics
Step by Step Guide and Essential Practice with Answers
MathFlare Publishing

MathFlare
Grade 7
MATH WORKBOOK
Pre-Algebra
Ratio, Percent Proportion
Geometry
Statistics
Step by Step Guide and Essential Practice with Answers
MathFlare Publishing

MathFlare
Grade 7-8
MATH WORKBOOK
Pre-Algebra
Ratio, Percent Proportion
Geometry and Cartesian Plane
Statistics
Step by Step Guide and Essential Practice with Answers
MathFlare Publishing

MathFlare
Grade 8-9
MATH WORKBOOK
Pre-Algebra
Ratio, Proportion and Percentage
Linear Equations
Geometry and Cartesian Plane
Step by Step Guide and Essential Practice with Answers
MathFlare Publishing

MathFlare
Grade 8
MATH WORKBOOK
Pre-Algebra
Percentage
Linear Equations
Geometry
Step by Step Guide and Essential Practice with Answers
MathFlare Publishing

Order of Operations (PEMDAS)

The order of operations, often remembered by the acronym PEMDAS, stands for:

- **Parentheses**: Perform operations inside parentheses first.
- **Exponents**: Evaluate exponents (powers and roots) next.
- **Multiplication and Division**: Perform multiplication and division from left to right.
- **Addition and Subtraction**: Perform addition and subtraction from left to right.

The order of operations helps to clarify which operations should be performed first in a mathematical expression to ensure consistent and accurate results.

- **Parentheses**: Evaluate expressions within parentheses first. If there are nested parentheses, start with the innermost ones and work your way out.

    1. Example: $2 \times (3 + 4) = 2 \times 7 = 14$

- **Exponents**: Evaluate expressions with exponents (powers and roots) next.

    1. Example: $2^3 + 4 = 8 + 4 = 12$

- **Multiplication and Division**: Perform multiplication and division from left to right.

    1. Example: $2 \times 3 + 4 = 6 + 4 = 10$

    2. Example: $6 \div 2 \times 3 = 3 \times 3 = 9$

- **Addition and Subtraction**: Perform addition and subtraction from left to right.

    1. Example: $2 + 3 \times 4 = 2 + 12 = 14$

    2. Example: $10 - 4 \div 2 = 10 - 2 = 8$

Solving Two-Step Equations

Solving two-step equations involves finding the value of the variable that makes the equation true. In a two-step equation, two operations (addition, subtraction, multiplication, or division) are performed on the variable.

The goal is to isolate the variable on one side of the equation by performing inverse operations in the reverse order of operations.

For example:

Given the equation $18 = (10 + b) - 2$, where we want to solve for b.

To solve for b, we need to undo the operations that have been performed on b.

1. Undo the subtraction by adding 2 to both sides:

$$18 + 2 = (10 + b) - 2 + 2$$

$$20 = 10 + b$$

2. Undo the addition by subtracting 10 from both sides:

$$20 - 10 = 10 + b - 10$$

$$10 = b$$

So, the solution to the equation is $b = 10$

Let's substitute $b = 10$ back into the original equation to verify if it satisfies the equation:

Original equation:

$$18 = (10 + b) - 2:$$

Substitute b = 10:

$$18 = (10 + 10) - 2$$

simplify:

$$18 = 20 - 2$$

$$18 = 18$$

Since the equation simplifies to 18 =1 8, it confirms that our solution b = 10 is correct.

Solving Multi-Step Equations

Solving multi-step equations involves finding the value of the variable that makes the equation true. In a multi-step equation, multiple operations (addition, subtraction, multiplication, or division) are performed on the variable.

The goal is to isolate the variable on one side of the equation by performing inverse operations in the reverse order of operations.

Example:

Given the equation $-3m - m = -8$, where we want to solve for m.

To solve for m, we need to undo the operations that have been performed on m.

1. Combine like terms on the left side:

$$-3m - m = -4m$$

2. Substitute the combined term back into the equation:

$$-4m = -8$$

3. Undo the multiplication by dividing both sides by −4−4:

$$\frac{-4m}{-4} = \frac{-8}{-4}$$

$$m = 2$$

Let's substitute m = 2 back into the original equation to verify if it satisfies the equation:

Original equation:

$$-3m - m = -8$$

Substitute m = 2:

$$-3(2) - 2 = -8$$

simplify:

$$-6 - 2 = -8$$

$$-8 = -8$$

Since the equation simplifies to 8 = 8, it confirms that our solution m = 2 is correct.

Equations (Two Sides)

A two-sided equation is an equation where both sides have expressions with variables and constants. The goal when solving a two-sided equation is to find the value of the variable that makes both sides equal.

For example: Let's solve an equation:

$$9 + 8x + 8 = 64 + x + 2$$

- **Combine Like Terms:** Simplify each side of the equation by combining like terms (terms with the same variable or constants).

$$9 + 8x + 8 = 64 + x + 2$$

$$17 + 8x = 66 + x$$

- **Isolate the Variable:** Use inverse operations to isolate the variable on one side of the equation.

subtract x from both sides:

$$17 + 8x - x = 66 + x - x$$

$$17 + 7x = 66$$

subtracting 17 from both sides:

$$17 - 17 + 7x = 66 - 17$$

$$7x = 49$$

divide both sides by 7:

$$\frac{7x}{7} = \frac{49}{7} = x = 7$$

- **Check Solution:** Once you find the solution, substitute it back into the original equation to ensure it makes the equation true.

Substitute $x = 7$ back into the original equation:

$$9 + 8(7) + 8 = 64 + 7 + 2$$

$$9 + 56 + 8 = 64 + 7 + 2$$

$$73 = 73$$

Simplifying expressions

It involves combining like terms and performing operations to make the expression easier to understand and work with.

Let's simplify the expression:

$$2x - 2x + 8 + 4$$

- **Combine like terms:** First, we look for terms with the same variable and exponent. In this expression, $2x$ and $-2x$ are like terms, so they can be combined:

$$2x - 2x = 0$$

- **Substitute the simplified terms:** After combining the like terms, the expression becomes:

$$0 + 8 + 4$$

- **Combine the remaining terms:** Now, we add the constants together:

$$8 + 4 = 12$$

Let's solve another problem:

$$-7m - 3 - 3 - 6m$$

combine like terms

$$-7m - 6m - 3 - 3$$

$$13m - 6$$

Evaluate Expressions

Evaluating expressions involves substituting given values for variables in an expression and then performing the indicated operations to find the result.

For example: Let's evaluate 4x – 10, when x = 3:

Step 1: Substitute the given value for the variable:

Replace every occurrence of x in the expression 4x – 10 with the given value, which is 3:

$$= 4(3) - 10$$

Step 2: Perform the operations:

Perform the indicated operations according to the order of operations (PEMDAS - Parentheses, Exponents, Multiplication and Division, Addition and Subtraction):

$$= 4 \times 3 - 10$$

Step 3: Simplify:

Calculate the result:

$$12 - 10 = 2$$

Linear Equation

A linear equation is an algebraic equation that represents a straight line when graphed on a coordinate plane. It consists of variables raised to the power of 1 (i.e., no exponents higher than 1) and constant coefficients.

The general form of a linear equation in one variable x is:

$$ax + b = 0$$

Where a and b are constants, and x is the variable.

Let's solve the linear equation:

$$-2x + 9 = 5$$

- **Isolate the variable term:** We want to isolate the term containing x on one side of the equation. To do this, we'll move the constant term to the other side. Subtract 9 from both sides:

$$-2x + 9 - 9 = 5 - 9$$

$$-2x = -4$$

- **Divide by the coefficient of the variable:** To solve for x, divide both sides by the coefficient of x, which is -2:

$$\frac{-2x}{-2} = \frac{-4}{-2}$$

$$x = 2$$

Quadratic Equations

A quadratic equation is a polynomial equation of the second degree, meaning it can be written in the form:

$$ax^2 + bx + c = 0$$

where a, b, and c are constants, and x is the variable being solved for. The solutions to a quadratic equation are the values of x that make the equation true.

Now, let's solve the quadratic equation $11x^2 - 1 = 0$ and understand it step by step using quadratic formula.

1. **Identify the coefficients:**

   In the equation $11x^2 - 1 = 0$,

   $$a=11, b=0, \text{ and } c=-1.$$

2. **Apply the quadratic formula:**

   The quadratic formula states that for an equation $ax^2 + bx + c = 0$, the solutions for x are given by:

   $$x = \frac{-b \pm \sqrt{b^2 - 4ac}}{2a}$$

   Plugging in the values $a=11, b=0,$ and $c=-1$ into the quadratic formula, we get:

   $$x = \frac{-0 \pm \sqrt{0 - 4(11)(-1)}}{2(11)}$$

3. Simplify inside the square root:

$$0^2 - 4(11)(-1) = 0 - (-44) = 44$$

4. Plug in the simplified values:

$$x = \frac{\pm \sqrt{44}}{22}$$

5. Simplify the square root:

Since 44 is not a perfect square, we can write it as $\sqrt[2]{11}$

$$x = \frac{\pm \sqrt[2]{11}}{22}$$

6. Simplify further if possible:

We can simplify $\sqrt[2]{11}$ to $\sqrt{11}$ by canceling out the common factor:

$$x = \frac{\pm \sqrt{11}}{11}$$

7. Final solution:

So, the solutions to the equation are:

$$x = \frac{\sqrt{11}}{11} \text{ and } x = \frac{-\sqrt{11}}{11}$$

or

$$(x = 0.302, \text{ and } x = -0.302)$$

These are the roots of the quadratic equation. They represent the points where the graph of the quadratic equation intersects the x-axis.

Let's solve another equation:

$$-4p^2 + 6p - 6 = 0$$

$$p = \frac{-b \pm \sqrt{b^2 - 4ac}}{2a}$$

where $a = -4$, $b = 6$, and $c = -6$.

Let's plug these values into the quadratic formula:

$$p = \frac{-6 \pm \sqrt{6^2 - 4(-4)(-6)}}{2(-4)}$$

First, let's simplify inside the square root:

$$6^2 - 4\,(-4)\,(-6)$$

$$= 36 - 96 = -60$$

So, we have:

$$p = \frac{-6 \pm \sqrt{-60}}{-8}$$

We can simplify the square root of −60 by factoring out −1:

$$\sqrt{-60}$$

$$= \sqrt{-1 \times 60}$$

$$= \sqrt{-1} \times \sqrt{60}$$

$$= i\sqrt{60}$$

So, we have:

$$p = \frac{-6 \pm i\sqrt{60}}{-8}$$

Simplify:

$$\sqrt{60} \text{ to } \sqrt{4 \times 15} = 2\sqrt{15}$$

$$p = \frac{-6 \pm i \times 2\sqrt{15}}{-8}$$

Now, divide both the numerator and denominator by −2 to simplify:

$$p = \frac{3 \pm i\sqrt{15}}{4}$$

So, the solutions to the equation are:

$$p = \frac{3 + i\sqrt{15}}{4} \text{ and } p = \frac{3 - i\sqrt{15}}{4}$$

This equation -4p² + 6p - 6 = 0 has no real solutions.

When a quadratic equation has no real solutions, it means that the solutions are not real numbers, but rather complex numbers. In this case, the solutions involve the imaginary unit i because the discriminant (b^2-4ac) is negative, which results in taking the square root of a negative number when applying the quadratic formula.

In mathematics, such equations are said to have "no real roots" or "no real solutions." They are also sometimes referred to as having "complex roots" or "complex solutions." Complex numbers include a real part and an imaginary part, and they are often written in the form $a + bi$, where a and b are real numbers and i is the imaginary unit, defined as $i = \sqrt{-1}$.

Let's solve another equation:

$$12x^2 + 6x - 2 = 0$$

$$x = \frac{-b \pm \sqrt{b^2 - 4ac}}{2a}$$

where $a = 12$, $b = 6$, and $c = -2$.

Let's plug these values into the quadratic formula:

$$x = \frac{-6 \pm \sqrt{6^2 - 4(12)(-2)}}{2(12)}$$

First, let's simplify inside the square root:

$$6^2 - 4(12)(-2)$$

$$= 36 - (-96)$$

$$= 36 + 96$$

$$= 132$$

So, we have:

$$X = \frac{-6 \pm \sqrt{132}}{24}$$

Now, let's simplify the square root of 132:

$$X = \frac{-6 \pm \sqrt{4 \times 33}}{24}$$

$$X = \frac{-6 \pm 2\sqrt{33}}{24}$$

$$X = \frac{-6 \pm \sqrt{33}}{12}$$

So, the solutions to the equation are:

$$X = \frac{-6 + \sqrt{33}}{12} \text{ and } X = \frac{-6 - \sqrt{33}}{12}$$

or (x = 0.229, and x = -0.729)

Let's solve a quadratic equation where the right side is a number, instead of 0.

$$-8n^2 + 6n + 30 = 7$$

To solve the equation, we first need to bring all terms to one side to set the equation equal to zero:

$$-8n^2 + 6n + 30 - 7 = 0$$

Simplify:

$$-8n^2 + 6n + 23 = 0$$

Now, to solve for n, we can use the quadratic formula:

$$n = \frac{-b \pm \sqrt{b^2 - 4ac}}{2a}$$

where $a = -8$, $b = 6$, and $c = 23$.

Plugging these values into the formula, we get:

$$n = \frac{-6 \pm \sqrt{6^2 - 4(-8)(23)}}{2(-8)}$$

$$n = \frac{-6 \pm \sqrt{36 + 736}}{-16}$$

$$n = \frac{-6 \pm \sqrt{772}}{-16}$$

Now, let's simplify the square root of 772. We can factor out 4:

$$\sqrt{772} = \sqrt{4 \times 193} = 2\sqrt{193}$$

So, our equation becomes:

$$n = \frac{-6 \pm 2\sqrt{193}}{-8}$$

So, the solutions to the equation are:

$$n = \frac{-3 + \sqrt{193}}{-8} \quad \text{and} \quad n = \frac{-3 - \sqrt{193}}{-8}$$

or

(n = -1.362, and n = 2.112)

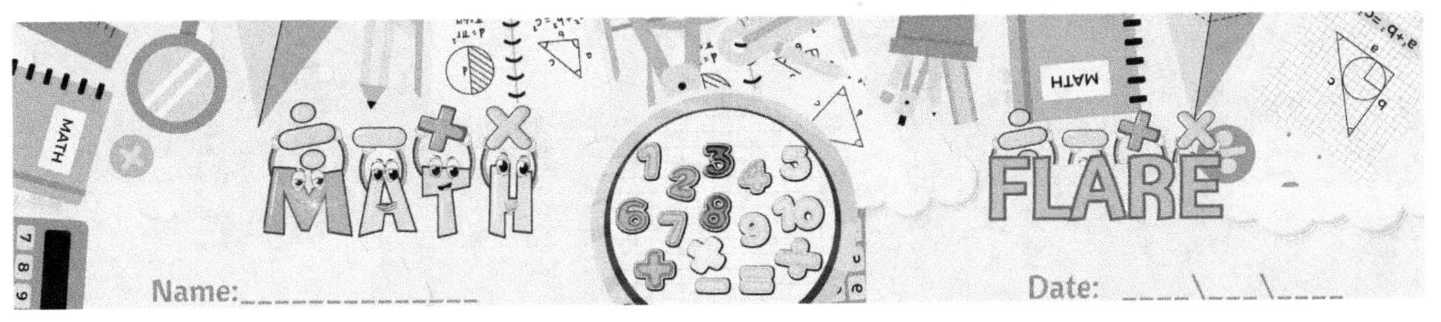

Order of Operations (PEMDAS)

1. $1(9 + 5) =$

2. $7 + 10^2 + 2 + 3^2 =$

3. $7 \times 2 + 3 =$

4. $3(4 + 4) =$

5. $7 + 8^2 + 3 + 9^2 =$

6. $3 + 8 + 4 =$

7. $(6 + 2)(4 + 6) =$

8. $(2 + 2)(3 + 10) =$

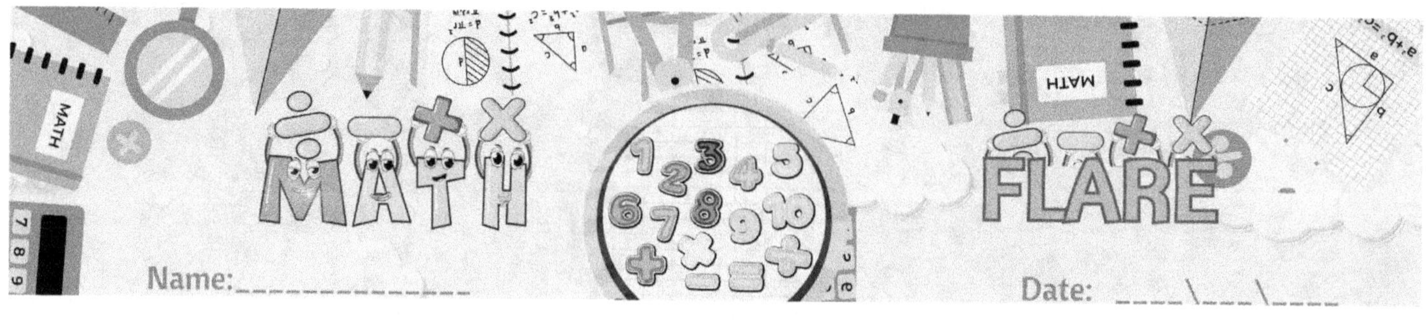

Name:___________________   Date: _______________

9. $7 \times 2 + 6 =$

10. $4 + 10 - 4 + 9 =$

11. $(1 + 6)^2 =$

12. $6 \times (5 + 1) =$

13. $(7 + 7) \div 6 =$

14. $5(3 + 10) =$

15. $6 + 7 + 2 =$

16. $5 \times 2 \times 1 =$

17. $(1 + 2) \times (10 + 10) =$

18. $6 + 9 - 5 + 8 =$

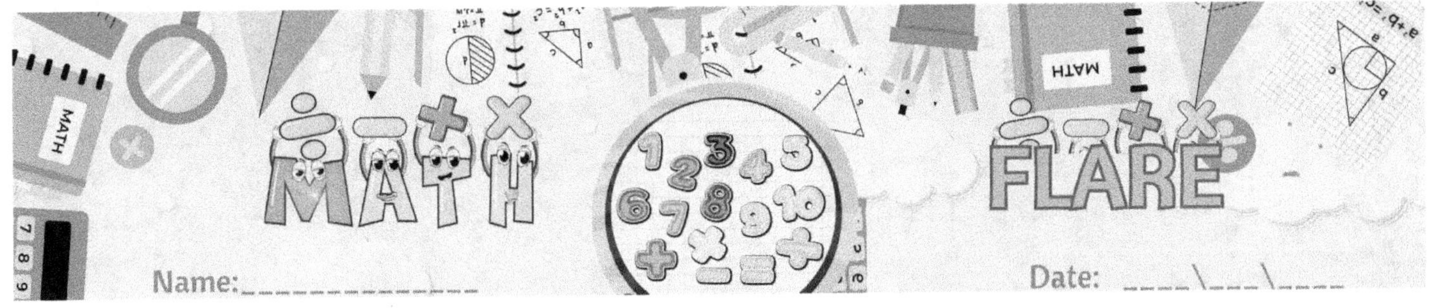

19. $10 + 3^2 + 1 + 10^2 =$

20. $8 + 10 + 4 =$

21. $10 \times (9 + 7) =$

22. $(7 + 3)^2 + (8 + 8)^2 =$

23. $7 + 10 + 6 =$

24. $(9 \times 4) - (3 + 6) =$

25. $7 \times 9 =$

26. $(2^2) \times (1^2) + 5 =$

27. $4 + 9 + 5 =$

28. $(9 + 6) \times (7 + 2) =$

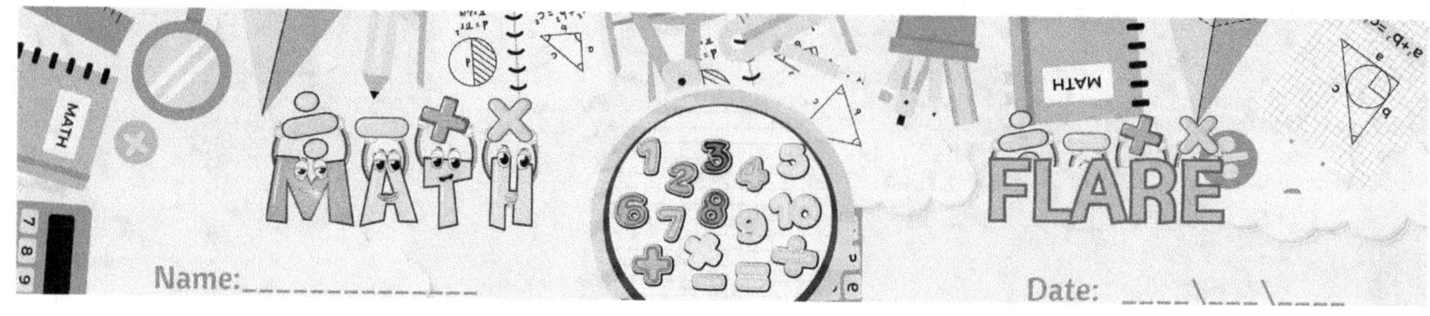

29. $8 \times 1 =$

30. $(4 + 7) \times (6 + 8) =$

31. $4 \times 7 + 7 =$

32. $8(5 + 8) =$

33. $(9 + 4)^2 + (3 + 5)^2 =$

34. $10 + 4 + 7 =$

35. $6 + 3^2 + 3 + 3^2 =$

36. $5 + 9 - 10 + 4 =$

37. $(6 + 6) \times (6 + 10) =$

38. $2 + 1^2 =$

39. $(2 + 1) \div 7 =$

40. $3(3 + 1) =$

41. $(2 + 10)^2 + (7 + 10)^2 =$

42. $9 + 5 + 4 =$

43. $(2 + 2) \times (2 + 4) =$

44. $(5 + 6)^2 + (9 + 2)^2 =$

45. $9 \times 6 =$

46. $(9 \times 9) - (8 + 6) =$

47. $5 + 8 + 1 =$

48. $1 + 9 + 3 =$

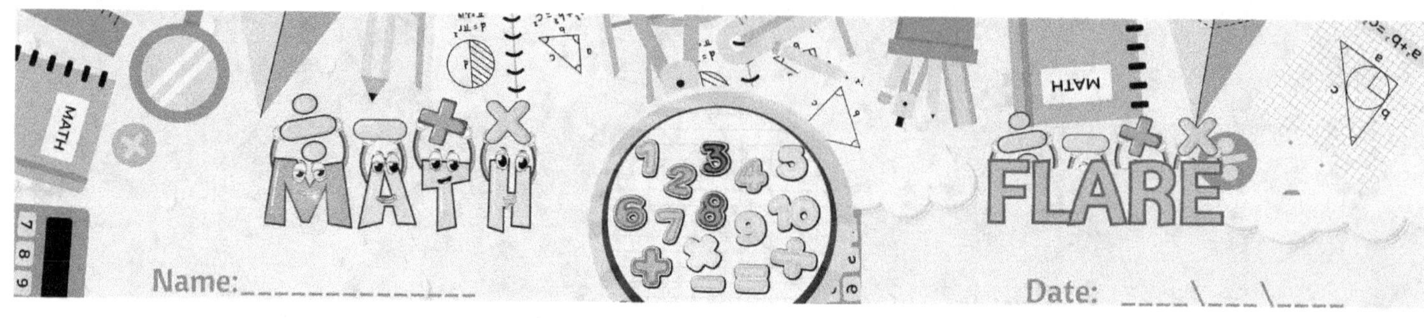

49. $8 + 7 + 3 =$

50. $6 + 2 - 8 + 4 =$

51. $6 \times 6 \times 6 =$

52. $(3 \times 5) - (1 + 6) =$

53. $(8 + 2)^2 + (5 + 2)^2 =$

54. $1 + 5 + 3 =$

55. $9 + 3 + 6 =$

56. $9 \times 5 + 5 =$

57. $5 \times 7 =$

58. $(2^2) \times (6^2) + 9 =$

59. $(1^2) \times (2^2) + 6 =$

60. $6 \times 9 + 6 =$

61. $2 + 8 + 3 =$

62. $4 + 7 + 3 =$

63. $(3 + 4) \div 8 =$

64. $(3 + 8) \times (3 + 4) =$

65. $9(10 + 4) =$

66. $1 + 10^2 + 4 + 8^2 =$

67. $(7 + 8)^2 =$

68. $3 \times 9 \times 9 =$

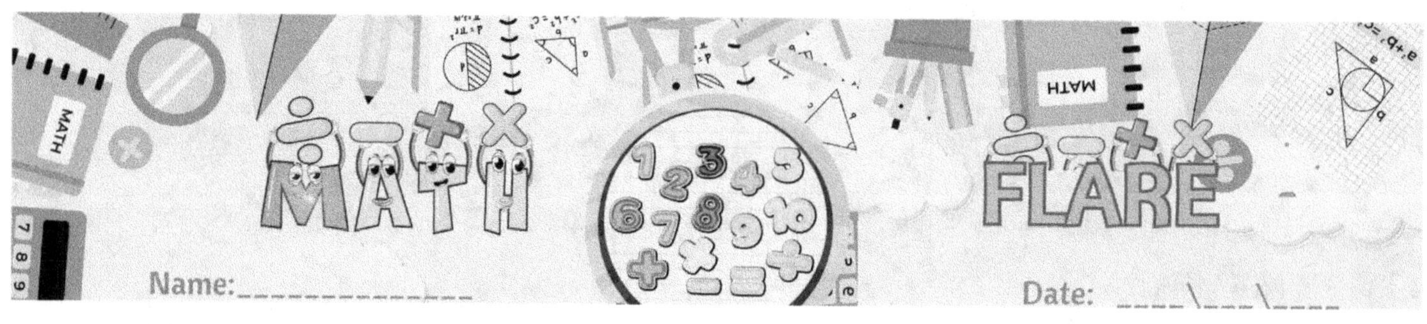

Solving Two-Step Equations

Solve for the variable.

1. $2 = 4 - \dfrac{z}{2}$

2. $(4 - y)6 = 0$

3. $8 = (1 + a) - 3$

4. $3 = (10 - x) - 5$

5. $4\dfrac{-m}{1} = -4$

6. $(3 + k)1 = 6$

7. $12 = (8 + a) - 1$

8. $\dfrac{9 + b}{5} = 3.8$

9. $10(9 + s) = 140$

10. $\dfrac{k}{-1} + 6 = 0$

11. $10(9 - x) = -10$

12. $9 + \dfrac{y}{1} = 19$

13. $80 = 8(1 + s)$

14. $10\dfrac{k}{1} = 10$

15. $\dfrac{z}{1} + 4 = 5$

16. $7 = 6 + \dfrac{b}{6}$

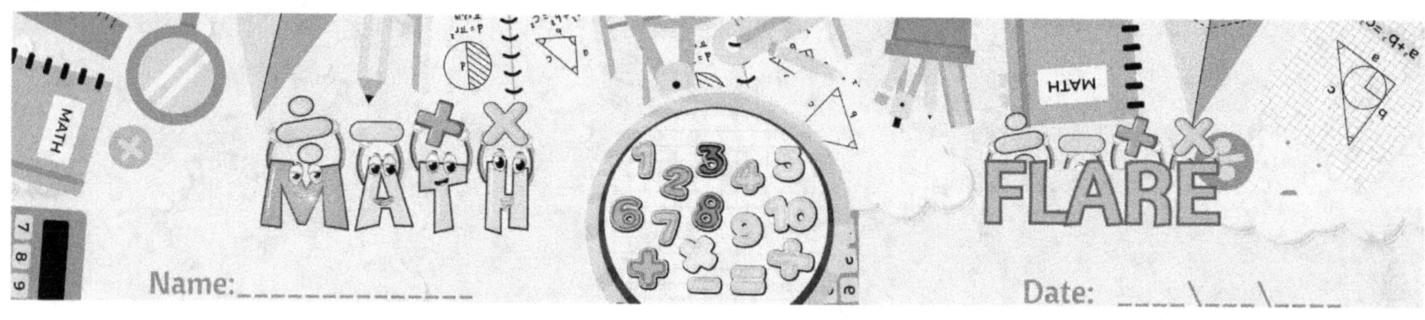

17. $-5 = (-2 + y) - 4$

18. $-72 = 9(-10 + z)$

19. $40 = 10\dfrac{a}{1}$

20. $19 = 7k + 5$

21. $\dfrac{8 + a}{2} = 9$

22. $18 = 9\dfrac{b}{5}$

23. $4 - \dfrac{b}{1} = 0$

24. $-48 = 8\dfrac{-m}{1}$

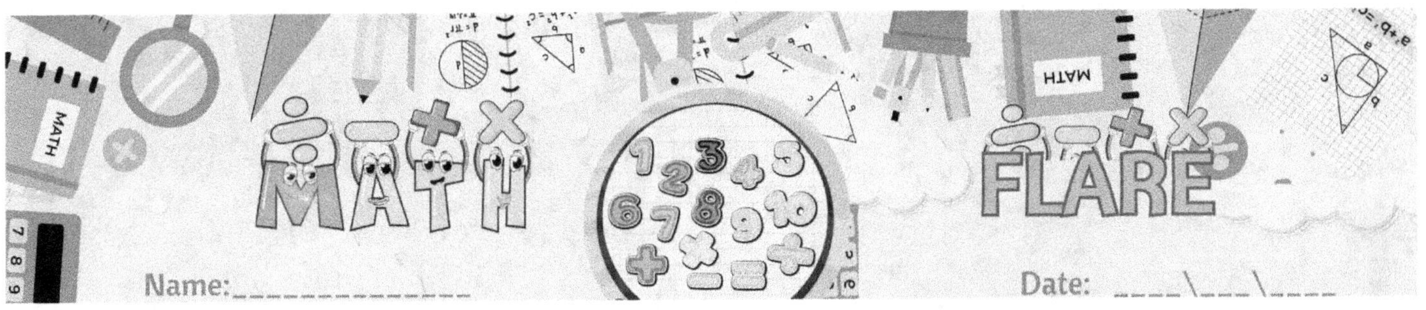

Name:________________   Date: _______________

25. $12 = -8 \dfrac{s}{-6}$

26. $(-4 + a) - 4 = 2$

27. $3 = -1(-10 + b)$

28. $-3 = 1 - \dfrac{k}{2}$

29. $10 + \dfrac{x}{2} = 12$

30. $(7 + y) - 9 = 0$

31. $5m + 2 = 12$

32. $6 \dfrac{-x}{2} = -24$

33. $0 = \dfrac{y}{9} - 1$

34. $(2 + k)8 = 88$

35. $(8 - z)2 = 14$

36. $-8 = -4z - 4$

37. $4(2 - x) = -12$

38. $\dfrac{-1 + a}{9} = 0.9$

39. $6(5 + z) = 84$

40. $-10 \dfrac{b}{-9} = 1.1$

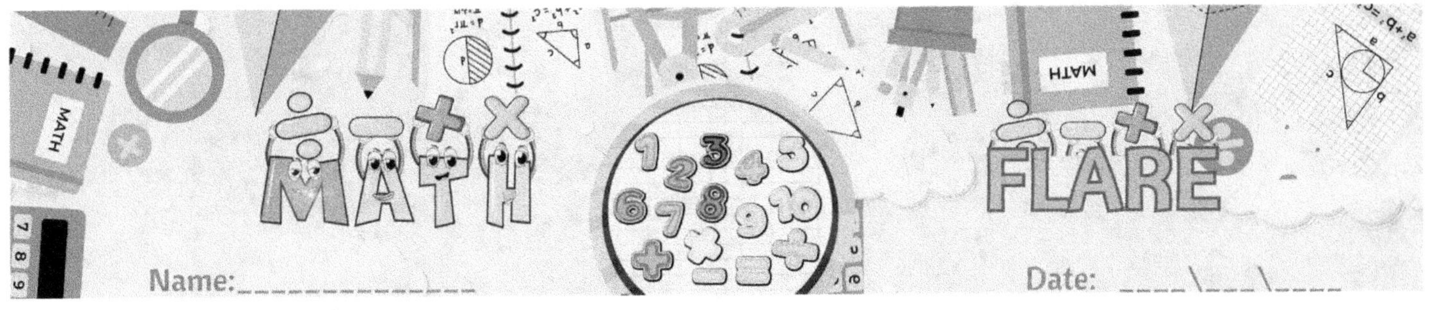

41. $m - 5 = 5$

42. $\dfrac{y}{6} + 1 = 2$

43. $6(-2 + k) = -6$

44. $6s - 9 = 15$

45. $8 + \dfrac{b}{1} = 18$

46. $-10 = 10\dfrac{-a}{10}$

47. $\dfrac{8 + z}{-8} = -1.5$

48. $-12 = -1(9 + m)$

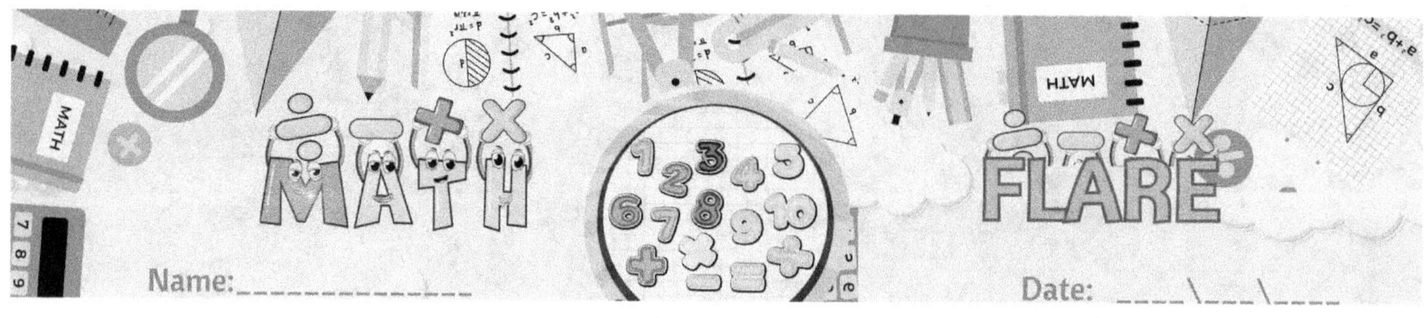

49. $3s + 9 = 12$

50. $-17 = -2y - 5$

51. $6 = -6(-7 + y)$

52. $(9 + z) - 1 = 14$

53. $8(5 - s) = -40$

54. $53 = 9m + 8$

55. $-6 = 6\dfrac{-x}{1}$

56. $-9y - 3 = -21$

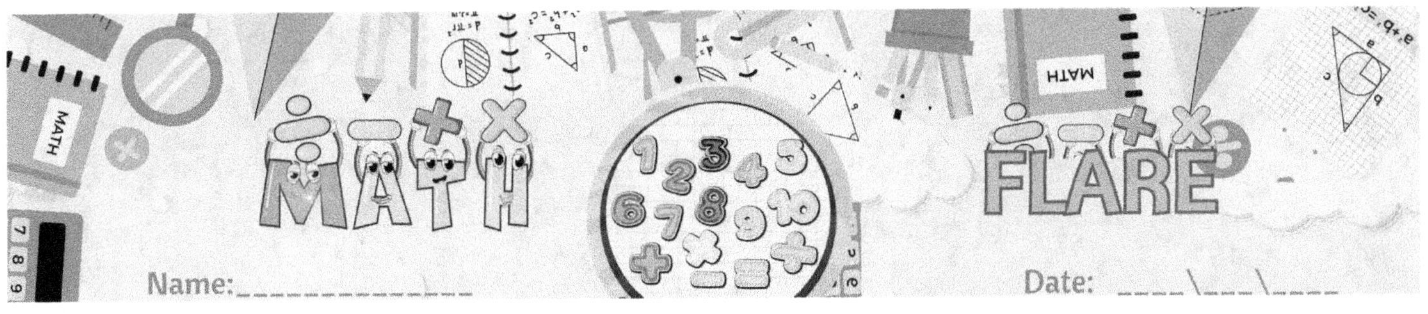

57. $2b - 1 = 11$

58. $-12 = 4 \dfrac{-y}{2}$

59. $(6 - m)3 = -9$

60. $13 = \dfrac{y}{2} + 8$

61. $9(-7 + a) = 0$

62. $28 = 6k + 4$

63. $-9(-8 + k) = 18$

64. $5 = \dfrac{z}{2} + 1$

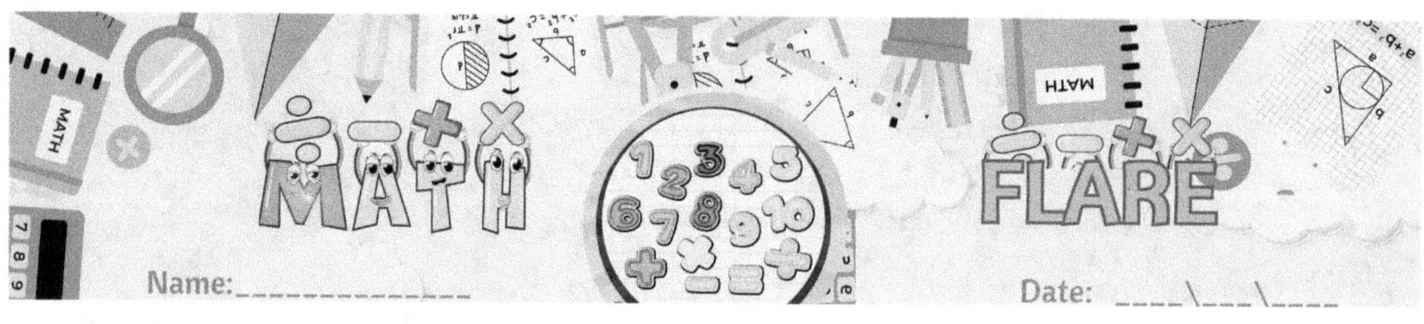

Solving Multi-Step Equations

Solve for the variable.

1. $-5 = -5y + 4y$

2. $-18 = -2k - 9 - k$

3. $-19 = -9 - 6m + 4m$

4. $-4 + 10a - 4 = 12$

5. $17 = -10 + 3b + 6$

6. $2 + z - 10z = -61$

7. $-12 = -9k + 4 + k$

8. $-40 = -3b - 8 - b$

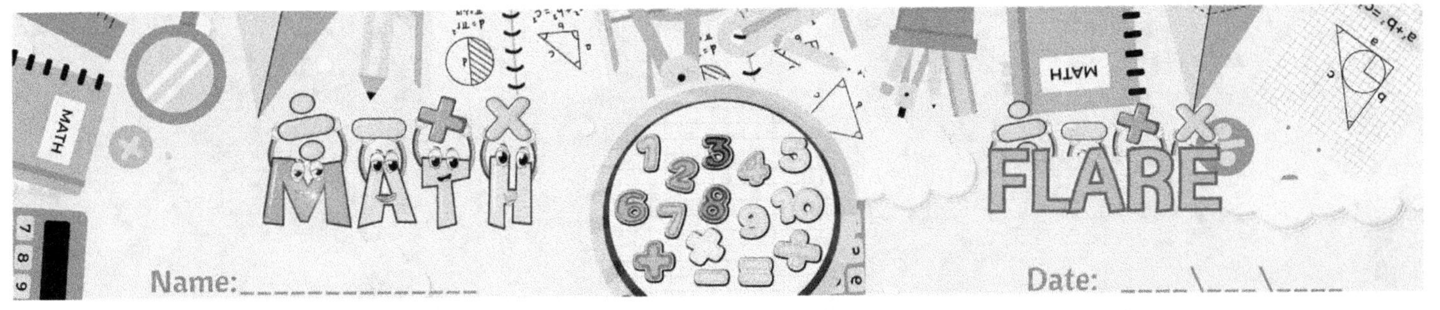

9. $37 = 1 + 6x + 6x$

10. $2s + 9 + s = 15$

11. $10 = 10 + 8x - 8x$

12. $-35 = b + 5 - 5b$

13. $12 = -s + 4 + 5s$

14. $s - 6 + s = 14$

15. $-3a + 2 + 6 = -22$

16. $27 = 6z - 8 - z$

17. $-6b + 3 - 10 = -43$

18. $-9x - x = -50$

19. $-9s + 2 - 8 = -15$

20. $2s + 3 + s = 27$

21. $-42 = m + 3 - 10m$

22. $10 + 6k - 2k = 38$

23. $8 - a - 7a = -40$

24. $-4 - m + 3m = 2$

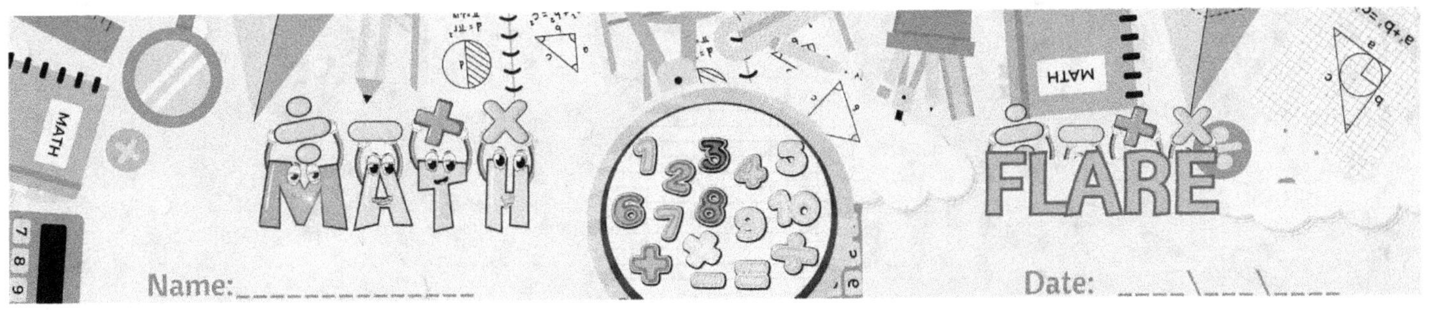

25. $2 = -5s + 4 + 8$

26. $-20 = 10 - z - 4z$

27. $-20 = 4 - k - 5k$

28. $-36 = -5a + a$

29. $-5x + 7x = 10$

30. $12 = -a + 7a$

31. $-21 = -9 - a - 3a$

32. $-21 = 9 - 8k - 6$

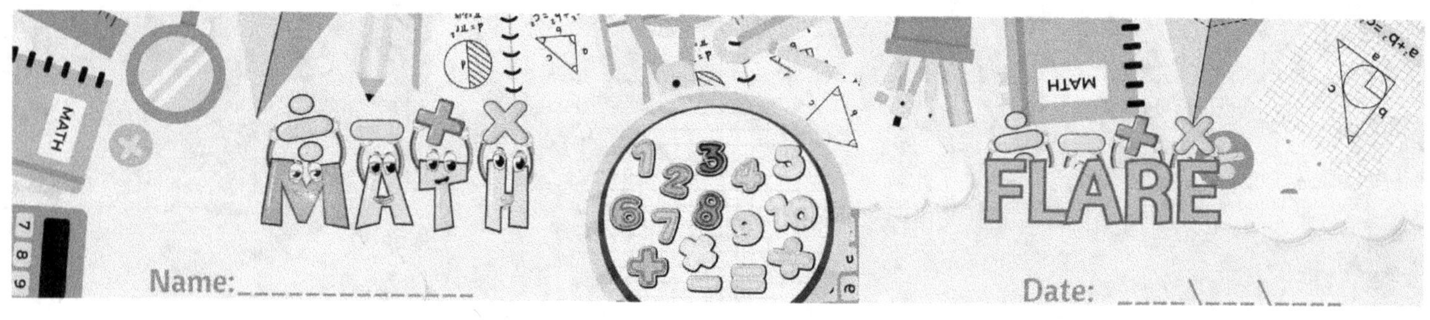

33. $-5 = -10 - y + 6y$

34. $-8b - b = -9$

35. $6a - 6a = 0$

36. $2a + 8 + a = 26$

37. $-8 - a - 8a = -53$

38. $-37 = 7 - y - 10y$

39. $-40 = -1 - 8s + 1$

40. $16 = y + 6 + 8$

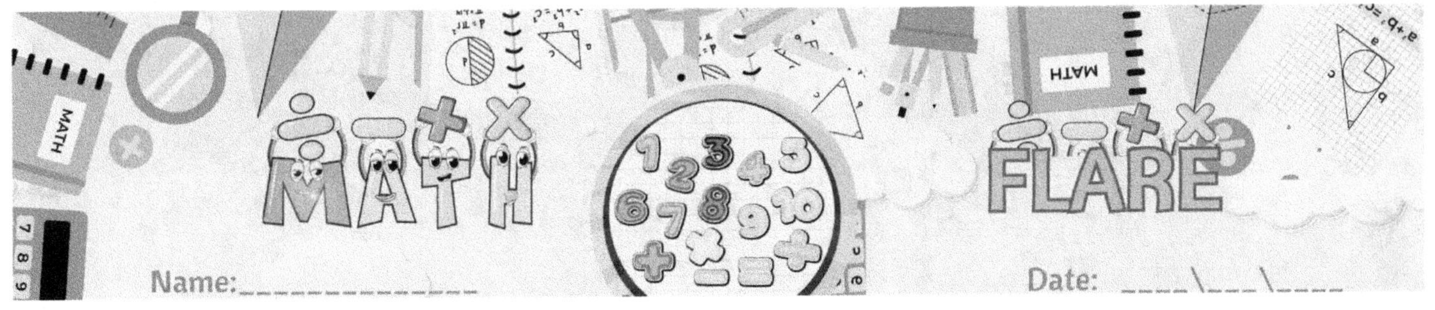

41. $k - 10 + 5k = 14$

42. $1 + s - 4s = -20$

43. $1 + m + m = 7$

44. $-64 = -5 - 8s - 3$

45. $-18 = a + 9 - 4a$

46. $-3m + m = -18$

47. $-52 = -10k - 8 - k$

48. $15 = 9a - 9 - a$

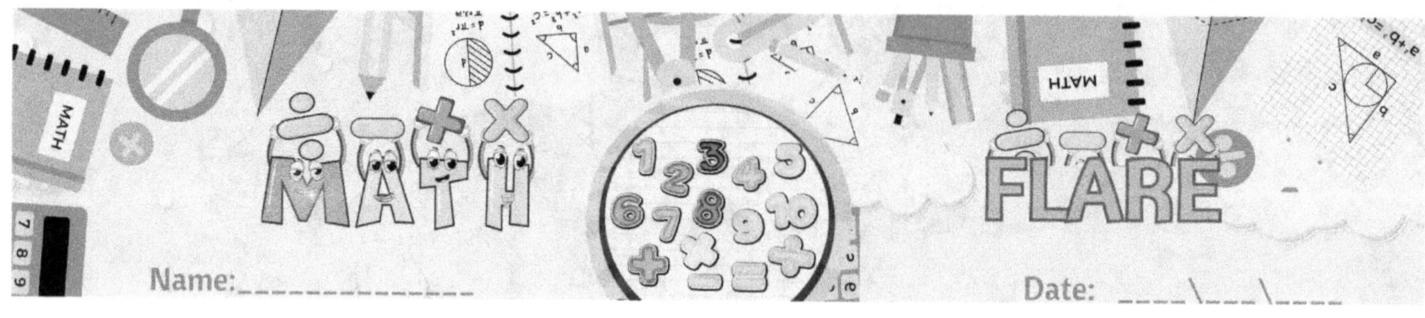

49. $-3x + x = -16$

50. $-1 - m - 5m = -49$

51. $-9y + 1 - 1 = -81$

52. $-8m + 2 + m = -40$

53. $53 = s - 2 + 10s$

54. $-7 = -4x + 3x$

55. $8x + 7 + 4 = 35$

56. $65 = 9m - 7 - m$

Equations (Two Sides)
Solve for the variable.

1. $27 - k = 1 + -4k + -1$

2. $-5 - z + -1 = -2 + -8z + 3$

3. $62 + k = 8 + -4k + 9$

4. $24 - s = 3s$

5. $6 + 2z + -7 = 6 + z$

6. $6 + 9s = 27 + 2s$

7. $-10 + 6x = 25 - x$

8. $-3 + 5z + -9 = 28 + z$

9. $2 + -7y + 2 = 12 + y$

10. $-2m + 5 = 8 - m$

11. $2z = 15 - z$

12. $2k = -8 + k$

13. $-9 + s = -8s$

14. $3 + 9k = -7k + -141$

15. $-40 - k = -6k$

16. $4k + -8 = -17 + 3k$

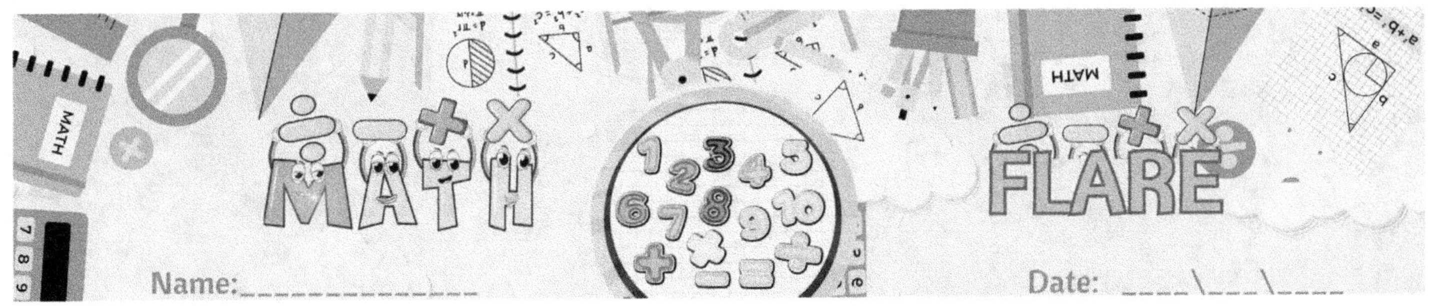

17. $9 + 9s = 6s + 21$

18. $-2k + 1 = 13 + k$

19. $-4 + a = -3a$

20. $1 + 4x + 10 = -10 + x$

21. $2 - -8b = 2b + -4$

22. $7 + 3y + -5 = 10 + y$

23. $5 + 8b = 19 + 6b$

24. $-3k = -14 - k$

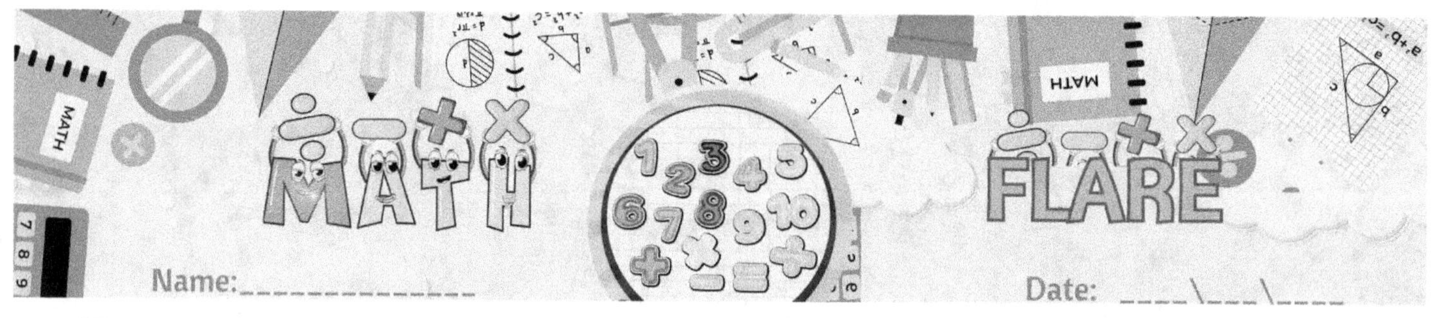

25. $2 + 8m + -7 = 2 + m$

26. $2k + 14 = 10 + 6k$

27. $-18 - k = 8k$

28. $-4x + 10 = -62 - -5x$

29. $-6x = 5 - x$

30. $-24 - s = 5s$

31. $4s + -2 = 7 + s$

32. $8k = 14 + k$

33. $4 + -3x = 32 + x$

34. $30 - s = 4s$

35. $40 - -3k = -10 + 8k$

36. $3 + 9z = 17 + 2z$

37. $1 + 2s = -5 - -5s$

38. $-24 - y = 3y$

39. $7 + 1a = 19 - -5a$

40. $-29 - 6b = 1 + 9b$

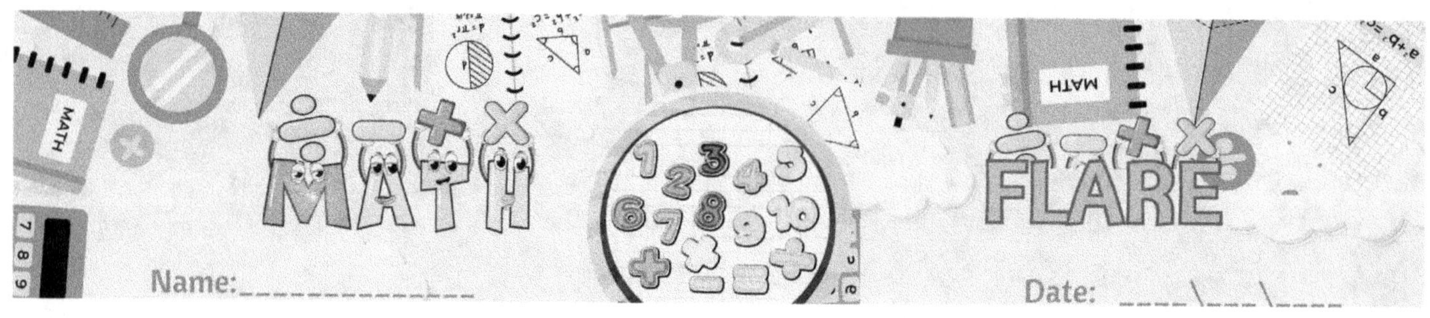

41. $-6 + 6x + -1 = 28 - x$

42. $5 + a = -4a$

43. $-17 + 3y = 7y + -1$

44. $2 + 2s = 20 - -8s$

45. $2a = 27 - a$

46. $9 - s = 8s$

47. $9k + -3 = -3 - -9k$

48. $75 - 2m = 9m + -2$

49. $-5 + 2s = 22 - s$

50. $-5m + 120 = -6 + 9m$

51. $32 + k = -3k$

52. $6 + y = -2y$

53. $10s + -4 = 30 - 7s$

54. $-9z + -10 = 0 + z$

55. $-9 + 10a = 36 + 5a$

56. $10 + 3m + -8 = 22 + m + -12$

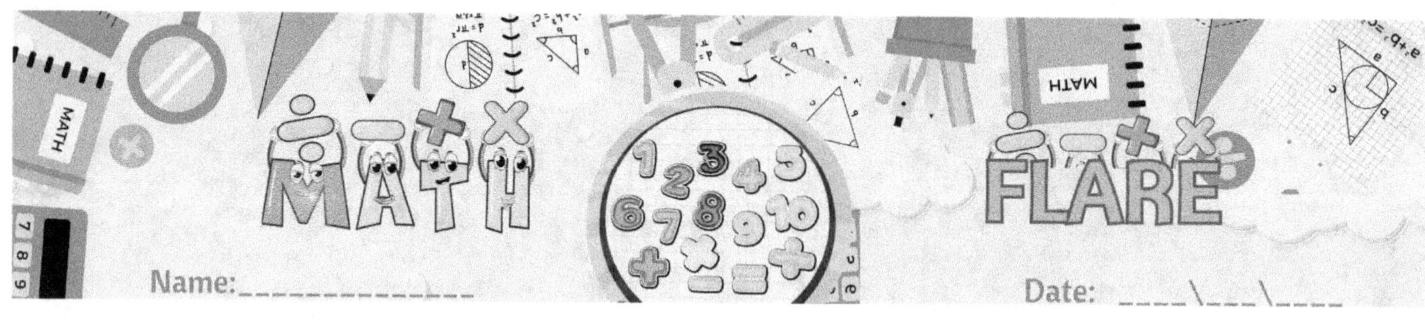

Simplify Expressions

1. $10x - 10 + 15x - 12 + 20x + 8$

2. $m + 19m$

3. $-x + 5x$

4. $19 + 10x - 17x + 15 - 7x$

5. $-17x + 12 + 7x$

6. $y - y$

7. $-17z + 12 - z$

8. $2 + 4k - 15k$

9. $20y + 20 - 3y + 8 + 14y + 19$

10. $2 + 11z - 15z + 15 - 14z$

11. $2 + 16y - 18y + 19 - 17y$

12. $11 - 2(16y - 6)$

13. $x + 16x$

14. $-14y - 20 - 20 - 6y$

15. $18m + 7 - 6 - 11m + 10m$

16. $9k + 2 - 9k + 16 + 2k + 3$

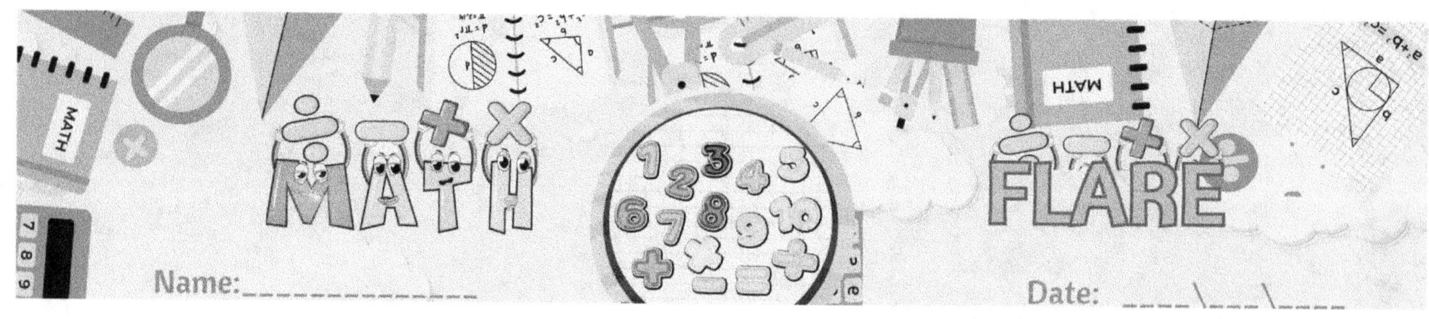

17. $-12m - 7m$

18. $15 + 17(7k - 4)$

19. $7 + 15(14m - 7)$

20. $-15y - y$

21. $x + 20x$

22. $17y - 12y + 3 + 17$

23. $-z - 17z$

24. $6 - 17(-10x + 16)$

25. 2 – 7(–15y + 14)

26. –7k + 20 + 6k + 14 + 17k – 3

27. –k – 20k

28. 13 + 2x – 16x

29. 8z + 2z

30. –13k + 10 + 20k + 16 + 15k – 20

31. 18k + 11 + 13k + 15 + 11k + 13

32. –8 + 10m – m – 15 – 4m

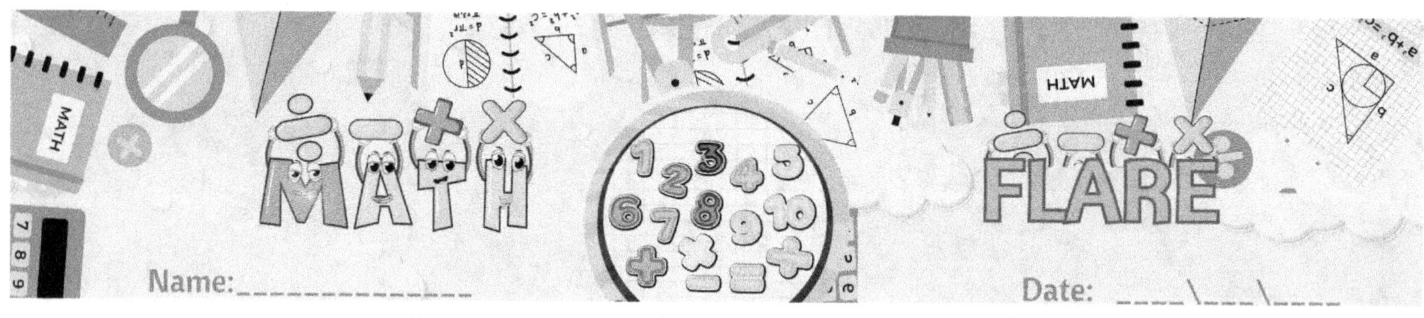

33. $-k + 9k + 16 - k$

34. $-6 + 1 - 16z + 2z - 1 + 3z$

35. $-12z + z$

36. $10x - 6x + 20 + 19$

37. $x - 10x + 2x + 14 + 4$

38. $4 + 8k + 7 + 6k$

39. $13m - 15 + 13m - 15 + 2m + 2$

40. $5 + 14y - 11y + 14 - 5y$

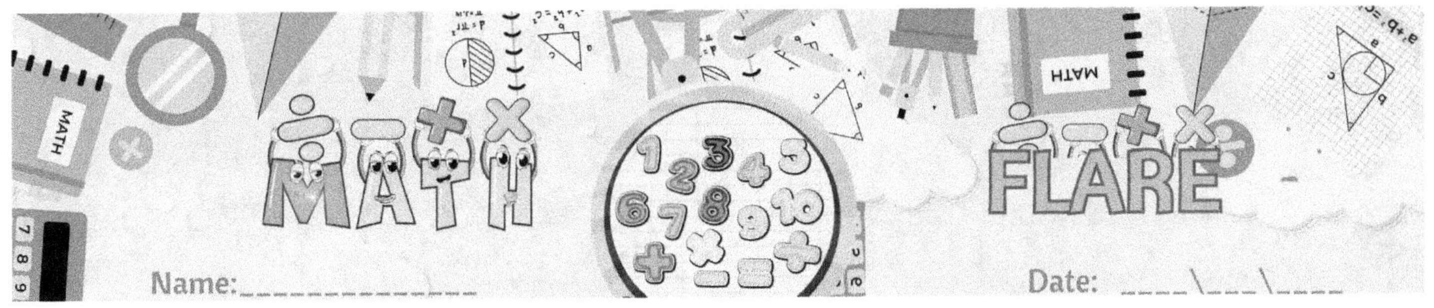

41. $-2x + 10 + 11x + 4 + 18x - 4$

42. $-15x - 8 + 3 - 2x$

43. $14k + 17 + 6k + 12 + 14k + 5$

44. $-14y - 4 - 6 - 6y$

45. $10 - 18x + 8 - 9x + 12 - 2x$

46. $-9k - 5 - 20k$

47. $5m - 13 - 5m + 4$

48. $-4x + x$

49. $8z - 13z + 12z - 1 + 3$

50. $5x - 3 - 6x + 6$

51. $-20 - 15z + 4z - 5 + 2z$

52. $-7 - 5z + 6z - 13 + 7z$

53. $14x + x$

54. $9 + 20(13y + 19)$

55. $9 + z - 19 + 16z$

56. $z + 13 + 18z$

57. $-17x + 3 + 10x + 9 + 16x - 3$

58. $-20k + k$

59. $2y - 10 - 12y + 18 - 19$

60. $-9m + 15m + 4 - 19m$

61. $10 - 12(-4x + 8)$

62. $5x + x$

63. $-5m - m$

64. $x + 4x$

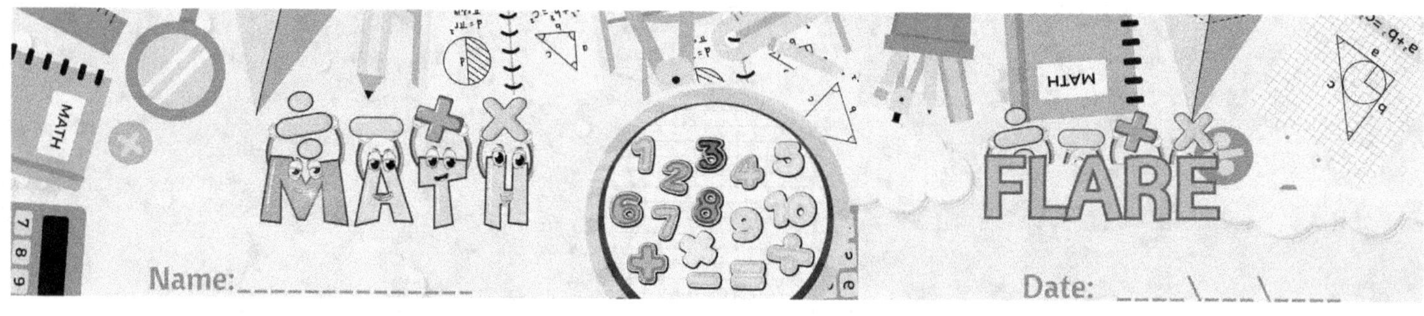

65. $8 + 12 + 4y - 15y + 13 - 16y$

66. $5 - 11(12m - 19)$

67. $18 + y - 3 + 7y$

68. $12x - x$

69. $-2 + 14y + 14 - 14y$

70. $-z - 5z$

71. $y - 11y$

72. $-3k + 19 + 18k + 10 + 15k - 19$

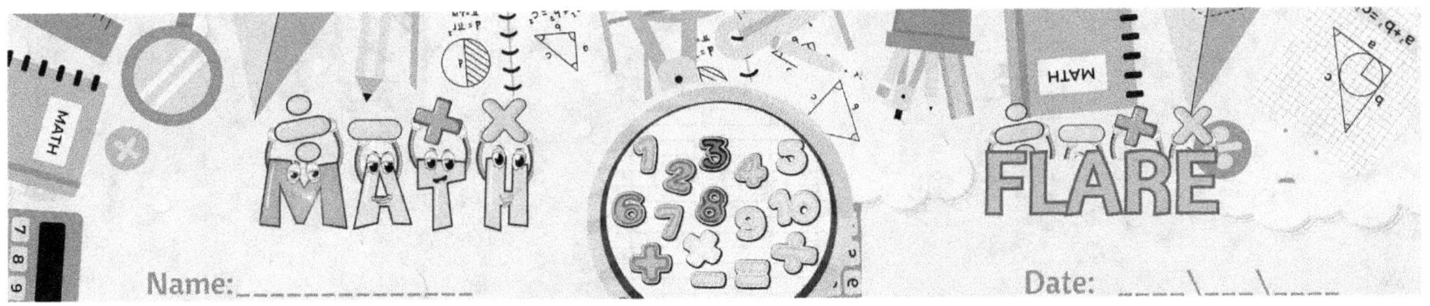

73. $-y - 18y$

74. $-8x + 5 - 16x$

75. $-10k - 13 + 8k$

76. $8 + k - 6 + k$

77. $6x - 6 + 3x - 9 + 2x + 3$

78. $m - 18m + 15m + 5 + 8$

79. $-z - 14z$

80. $-1 + 12y - 13y - 4 + 20y$

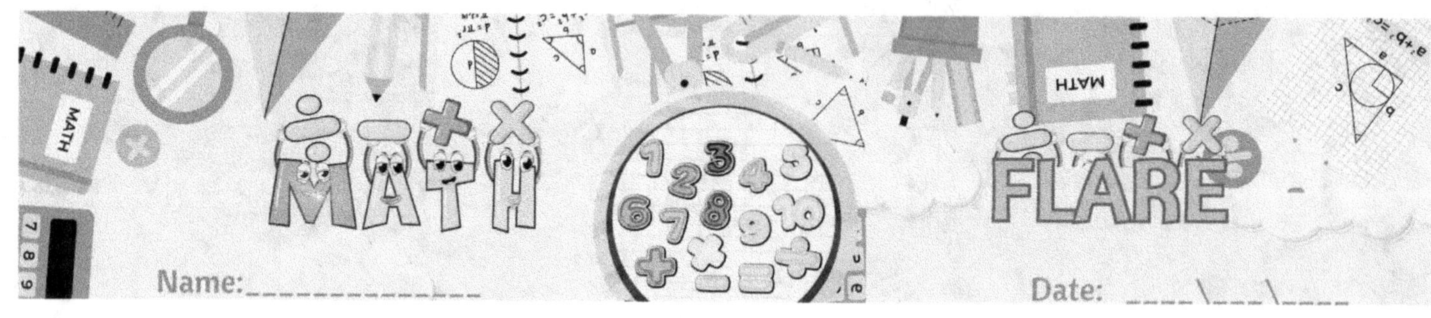

81. $-19y + 20 + 3y$

82. $-19y + y$

83. $-5x - 1 + 7 - 2x$

84. $12m - 10m + 17 + 7$

85. $14k - 2k$

86. $14m + 19m$

87. $1 + 13z - 17z + 13 - 16z$

88. $-11 + m - 15m - 10 + 6m$

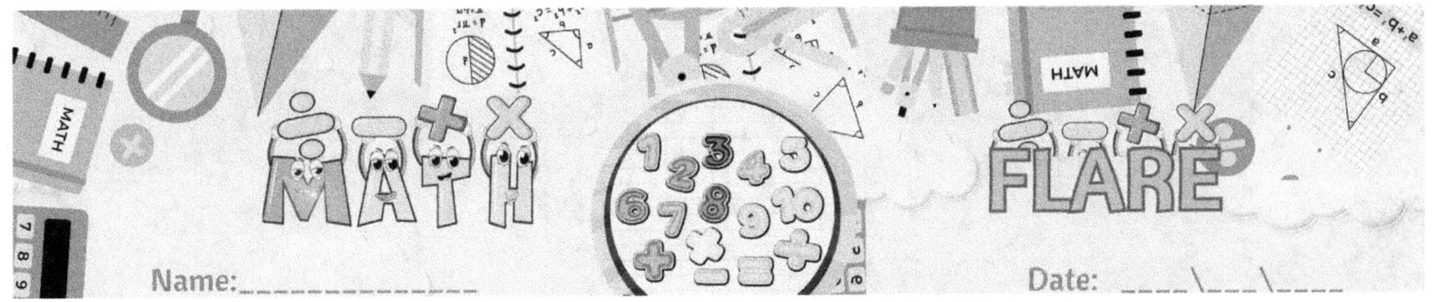

89. $3k - 19k + 3 + 5$

90. $2 + 18z - 14 + 12z - 14 + 14z$

91. $-6k + 18 + 14k + 19 + 19k - 11$

92. $-11 + 4m - 5m - 7 - 20m$

93. $2x + 9 + 20x + 20 + 13x + 7$

94. $-2z + 8 - 16z$

95. $9k - 11 - 20k + 16 - 4$

96. $6k + 20 + 11k + 11 + 19k + 19$

97. $18 + 3m + 5 + 20m$

98. $x - 2x + 17x + 12 + 3$

99. $-3k - 9 + 13 - 14k$

100. $20 - 7m + 10 - 7m + 2 - 5m$

101. $9 + 8 + 11x - 20x + 16 - 16x$

102. $-7 - 10z + 15 - 11z$

103. $3 + 18y - 3y + 3 - 14y$

104. $6k - 17k + 8 + 9$

Evaluating Equations

Simplify the following equations when the value of $n = -8$

1. $-7n + n =$

2. $2 - n =$

3. $5n - 10 =$

4. $n + 8 + (-2)n =$

5. $-2n^2 + (-1)n^3 =$

6. $-3 - n =$

7. $-3n - 6 + 6n =$

8. $-3(6 + n) =$

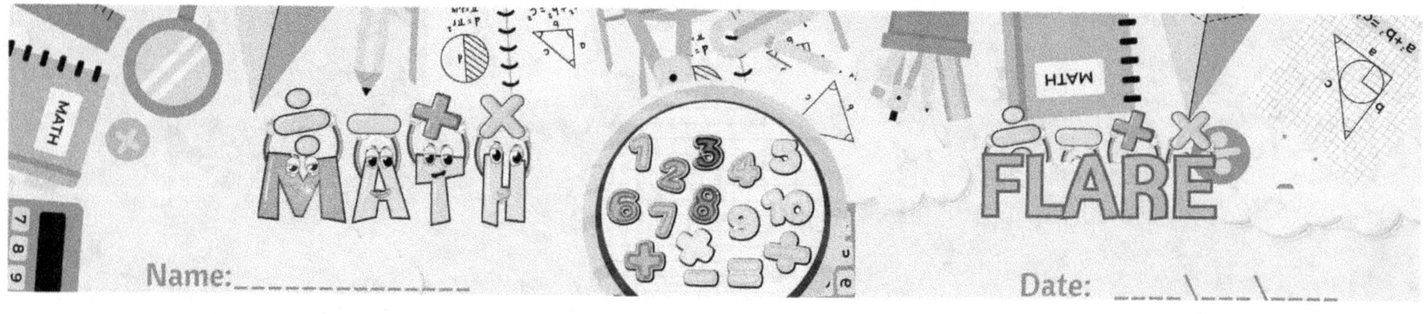

Name:________________   Date: _______________

Evaluating Equations

Simplify the following equations when the value of $n = 5$

1. $-9n - (-1) =$

2. $-2 + (-2n + (-7)) =$

3. $7 - n =$

4. $4n - (-2) =$

5. $n + 2 + 6n =$

6. $-6n - n =$

7. $n - (-5) =$

8. $-2n + (-1) =$

Evaluating Equations

Simplify the following equations when the value of $n = -5$

1. $0 - n =$

2. $10n + (-4) - n =$

3. $1 + 9n =$

4. $-2n^1 + (-10)n^3 =$

5. $-1n + n =$

6. $-9n - n =$

7. $(5 + 3n) + (n - 0) - (-10 + (-6)n) =$

8. $2(3 + n) =$

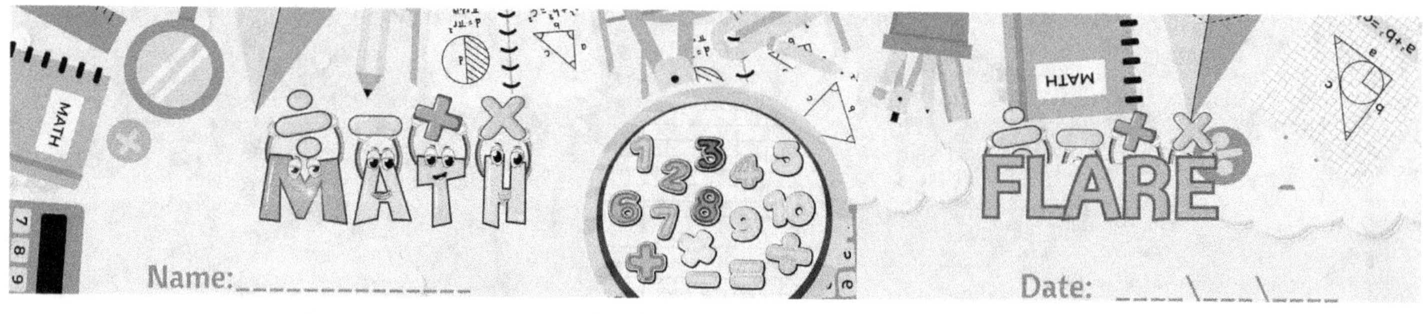

Evaluating Equations

Simplify the following equations when the value of $n = -3$

1. $7n + 0 =$

2. $7n + n =$

3. $n - 9 =$

4. $-5n + n =$

5. $-7 + (-8n + 9) - (-2) + (8n) =$

6. $-5 + (-8n + (-1)) =$

7. $-6n + 5 =$

8. $n - 6 =$

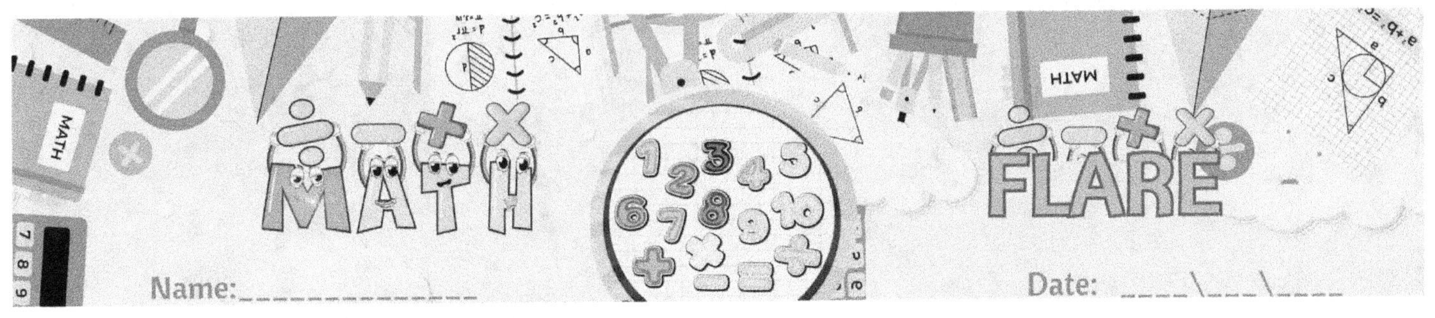

Evaluating Equations

Simplify the following equations when the value of n = -1

1. $2n - n =$

2. $(n^3 + 5) - (-4)(-3 + n) =$

3. $-1n + 8 =$

4. $(2n + 1) + (0n + 1) =$

5. $0n + n =$

6. $2n - (-7) =$

7. $-1 + (0n + (-2)) =$

8. $2(3 - n) =$

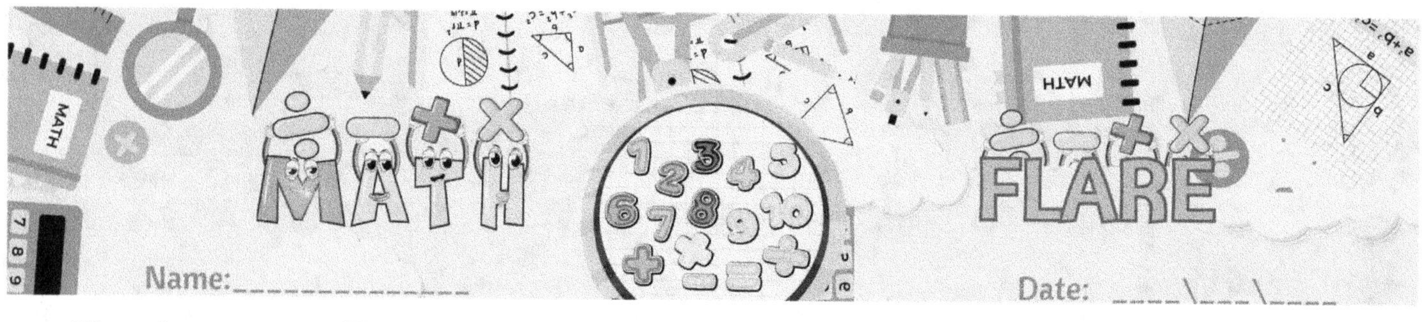

Evaluating Equations

Simplify the following equations when the value of n = 3

1. $-7n + 0 - 2n =$

2. $5n + (-8)n - 3 =$

3. $-2 + (4n + (-1)) - 7 + (2n) =$

4. $9 + (10n + 4) - 1 + (9n) =$

5. $3n + (-5) =$

6. $-7n + (-10) =$

7. $-7n - (-4) + (-8)n =$

8. $-5n + 0n + (-9)n =$

Evaluating Equations

Simplify the following equations when the value of n = -3

1. $-9(9 + n) =$

2. $n + 5 + (-2)n =$

3. $10 - n =$

4. $6n + 6 =$

5. $-10 - n =$

6. $n + 9 =$

7. $4n - (-3) =$

8. $3 + 10n =$

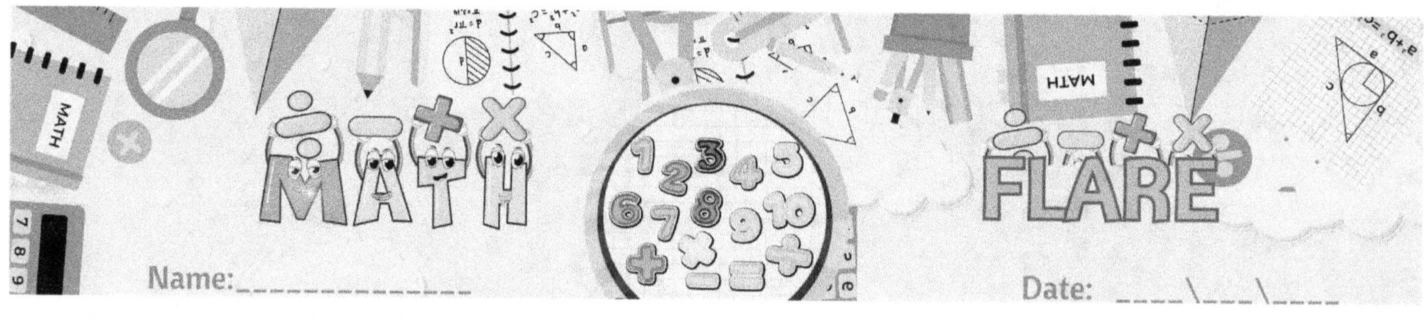

Evaluating Equations

Simplify the following equations when the value of n = -4

1. $n^1 + n - (-5) =$

2. $n + (-10) + 5n =$

3. $n + (-3) + 3n =$

4. $3(6 + n) =$

5. $3n + 7 - 7n =$

6. $-5^1 + n^3 =$

7. $0(-10 + n) =$

8. $8n + 7n + (-6)n =$

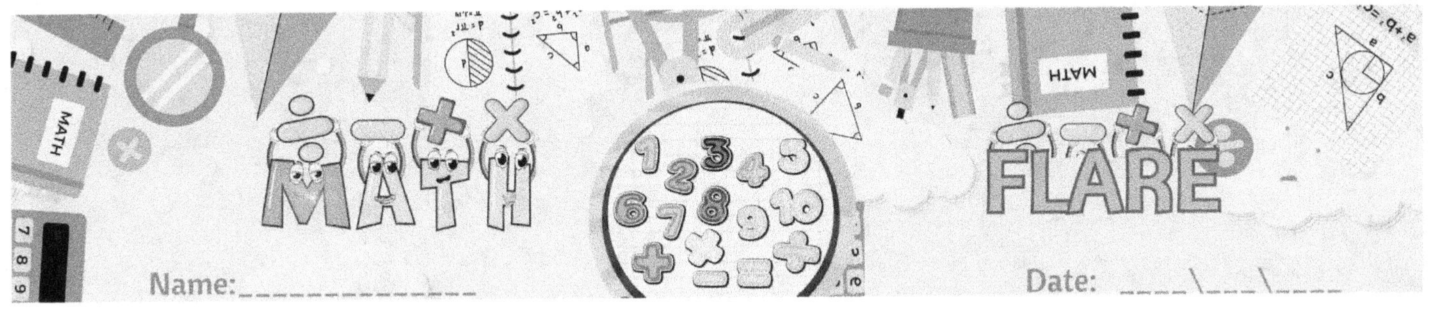

Evaluating Equations

Simplify the following equations when the value of $n = -10$

1. $-1n + (-1) =$

2. $-9 + (5n + 5) =$

3. $n + 0 =$

4. $(4 + n) + (n - (-3)) - (-5 + (-3)n) =$

5. $-8n + (-3) =$

6. $6 + (-4)n =$

7. $7 + n =$

8. $0n + (-3) =$

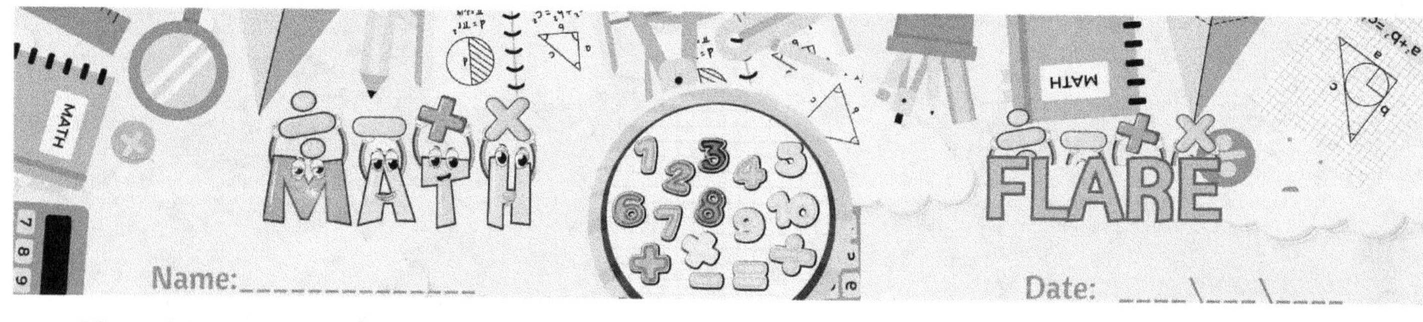

Evaluating Equations

Simplify the following equations when the value of $n = 4$

1. $-9(-1n - (-4)) + (-1)(-3 + n) =$

2. $-7^1 + n^3 =$

3. $-7 + (5n + 9) =$

4. $-9 + (-5)n =$

5. $5n + 5 =$

6. $-1n + (-4) =$

7. $0n + n =$

8. $(n^1 + 10) - 8(-5 + n) =$

Standard Linear Equations

1. $-4x + 2 = -6$

2. $-1x + 5 = 14$

3. $8x + -6 = 74$

4. $10x + -3 = 77$

5. $-10x + 1 = -69$

6. $5x + 1 = 21$

7. $-7x + -2 = -51$

8. $7x + -1 = -71$

9. $2x + 8 = 18$

10. $-4x + -9 = -49$

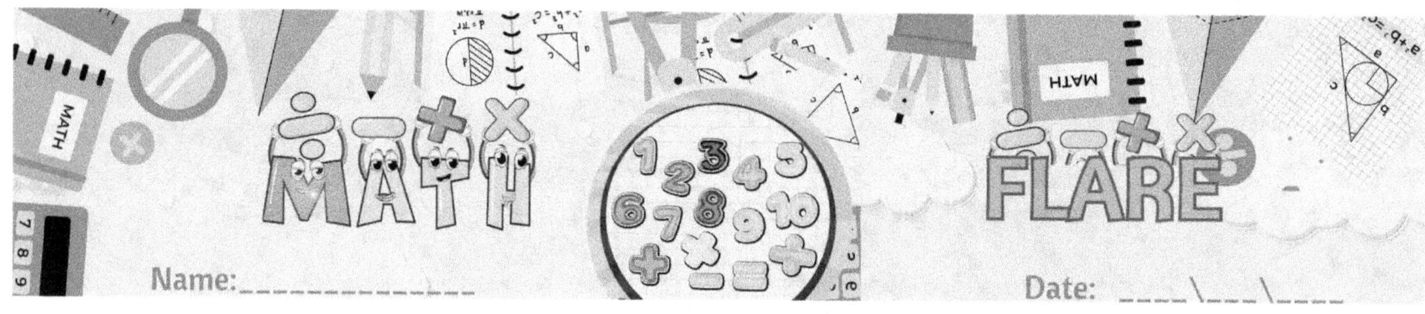

11. -1x + 9 = 6

16. -3x + 10 = 40

12. 4x + -2 = 30

17. 5x + -10 = -20

13. 10x + 2 = -78

18. -2x + 10 = 24

14. 10x + -7 = 93

19. 10x + -3 = -63

15. 5x + -8 = -58

20. -10x + -2 = -82

21. -5x + -10 = -55

26. -3x + -6 = -27

22. -5x + -7 = 23

27. -3x + -8 = -20

23. -2x + -3 = -1

28. -5x + -2 = 33

24. 3x + 0 = 0

29. -7x + -9 = 47

25. 9x + -5 = 85

30. -4x + 6 = 34

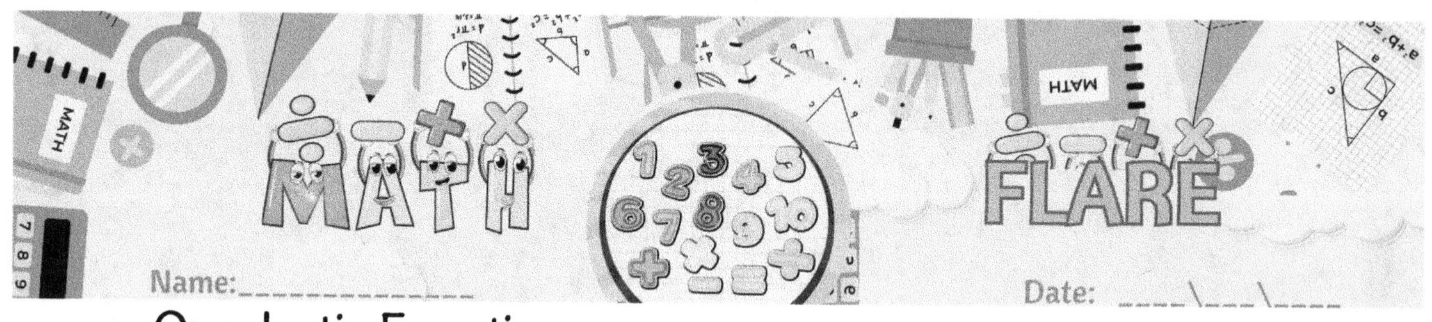

Quadratic Equations

1. $-b^2 + 10b + 11 = 0$

2. $6x^2 + 7x - 38 = 0$

3. $6r^2 - 22 = 0$

4. $5r^2 - r - 12 = 0$

5. $k^2 + 4k + 11 = 0$

6. $10n^2 + 5n - 11 = 0$

7. $-3r^2 + 12r + 15 = 0$

8. $3p^2 - 20 = 0$

9. $-5m^2 + 4m + 2 = 0$

10. $5m^2 - 13 = 0$

11. $2x^2 - 11x + 9 = 6$

16. $4p^2 + 12p - 140 = -5$

12. $2x^2 - 30 = -12$

17. $-5a^2 + 4a + 12 = 2$

13. $2n^2 - 10n - 90 = 10$

18. $p^2 - 37 = 12$

14. $2p^2 - 7p + 1 = -4$

19. $11m^2 - 11m + 4 = -5$

15. $-6x^2 + 4x + 108 = -4$

20. $-3a^2 - 10a + 55 = -2$

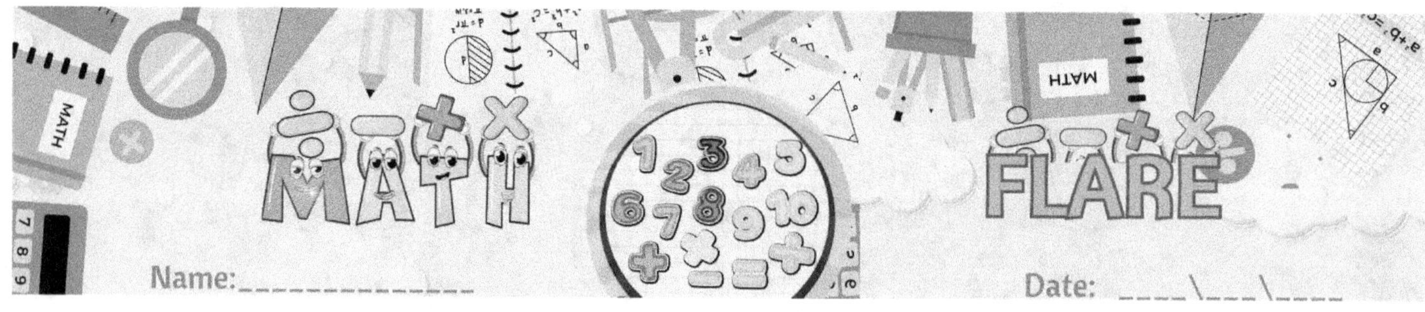

21. $-7x^2 = -24$

26. $10n^2 = 13$

22. $x^2 - 144 = 0$

27. $2a^2 = 50$

23. $v^2 = -8v + 13$

28. $-2n^2 - 9n = -81$

24. $9a^2 - 10 = 0$

29. $5 p^2 = 6 + p$

25. $2k^2 = 7 - 6k$

30. $6k^2 = 12 + 3k$

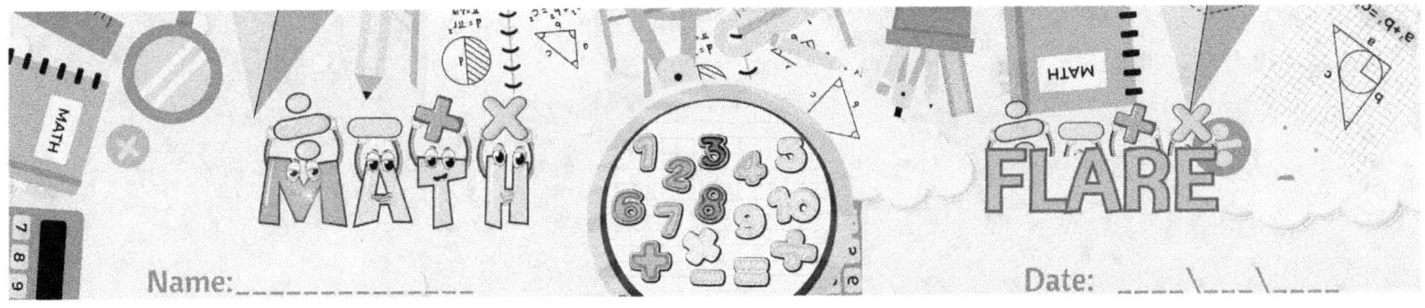

31. $4r^2 = 81$

36. $4r^2 = 1 + 3r$

32. $a^2 - 11a = 13$

37. $-3p^2 + 135 = 12p$

33. $-2m^2 + 19 = -8m$

38. $10a^2 = -5 + 3a$

34. $3v^2 - 10 = -7v$

39. $6r^2 = -7r + 55$

35. $-6x^2 = 11x + 4$

40. $n^2 + 15 = 10n$

ANSWERS

Page 1: Order of Operations (PEMDAS)

1. 14	2. 118	3. 17	4. 24	5. 155	6. 15	7. 80
8. 52	9. 20	10. 19	11. 49	12. 36	13. 2.3	14. 65
15. 15	16. 10	17. 60	18. 18	19. 120	20. 22	21. 160
22. 356	23. 23	24. 27	25. 63	26. 9	27. 18	28. 135
29. 8	30. 154	31. 35	32. 104	33. 233	34. 21	35. 27
36. 8	37. 192	38. 3	39. 0.4	40. 12	41. 433	42. 18
43. 24	44. 242	45. 54	46. 67	47. 14	48. 13	49. 18
50. 4	51. 216	52. 8	53. 149	54. 9	55. 18	56. 50
57. 35	58. 153	59. 10	60. 60	61. 13	62. 14	63. 0.9
64. 77	65. 126	66. 169	67. 225	68. 243		

Page 8: Solving Two-Step Equations

1. 4	2. 4	3. 10	4. 2	5. 1	6. 3	7. 5	8. 10
9. 5	10. 6	11. 10	12. 10	13. 9	14. 1	15. 1	16. 6
17. 1	18. 2	19. 4	20. 2	21. 10	22. 10	23. 4	24. 6
25. 9	26. 10	27. 7	28. 8	29. 4	30. 2	31. 2	32. 8
33. 9	34. 9	35. 1	36. 1	37. 5	38. 9	39. 9	40. 1
41. 10	42. 6	43. 1	44. 4	45. 10	46. 10	47. 4	48. 3
49. 1	50. 6	51. 6	52. 6	53. 10	54. 5	55. 1	56. 2
57. 6	58. 6	59. 9	60. 10	61. 7	62. 4	63. 6	64. 8

Page 16: Solving Multi-Step Equations

1. 5	2. 3
3. 5	4. 2
5. 7	6. 7
7. 2	8. 8
9. 3	10. 2
11. 4 or -199 or -198 or -197 or...	12. 10
13. 2	14. 10
15. 10	16. 7
17. 6	18. 5
19. 1	20. 8
21. 5	22. 7
23. 6	24. 3
25. 2	26. 6
27. 4	28. 9
29. 5	30. 2
31. 3	32. 3
33. 1	34. 1
35. 7 or -199 or -198 or -197 or...	36. 6
37. 5	38. 4
39. 5	40. 2

41. 4   42. 7

43. 3   44. 7

45. 9   46. 9

47. 4   48. 3

49. 8   50. 8

51. 9   52. 6

53. 5   54. 7

55. 3   56. 9

Page 23: Equations (Two Sides)

1. $k = -9$	2. $z = 1$	3. $k = -9$	4. $s = 6$	5. $z = 7$
6. $s = 3$	7. $x = 5$	8. $z = 10$	9. $y = -1$	10. $m = -3$
11. $z = 5$	12. $k = -8$	13. $s = 1$	14. $k = -9$	15. $k = 8$
16. $k = -9$	17. $s = 4$	18. $k = -4$	19. $a = 1$	20. $x = -7$
21. $b = -1$	22. $y = 4$	23. $b = 7$	24. $k = 7$	25. $m = 1$
26. $k = 1$	27. $k = -2$	28. $x = 8$	29. $x = -1$	30. $s = -4$
31. $s = 3$	32. $k = 2$	33. $x = -7$	34. $s = 6$	35. $k = 10$
36. $z = 2$	37. $s = 2$	38. $y = -6$	39. $a = -3$	40. $b = -2$
41. $x = 5$	42. $a = -1$	43. $y = -4$	44. $s = -3$	45. $a = 9$
46. $s = 1$	47. $k = 4$	48. $m = 7$	49. $s = 9$	50. $m = 9$
51. $k = -8$	52. $y = -2$	53. $s = 2$	54. $z = -1$	55. $a = 9$
56. $m = 4$				

Page 30: Simplify Expressions

1. 45x - 14
2. 20m
3. 4x
4. -14x + 34

5. -10x + 12
6. 0
7. -18z + 12
8. -11k + 2

9. 31y + 47
10. -18z + 17
11. -19y + 21
12. -32y + 23

13. 17x
14. -20y - 40
15. 17m + 1
16. 2k + 21

17. -19m
18. 119k - 53
19. 210m - 98
20. -16y

21. 21x
22. 5y + 20
23. -18z
24. 170x - 266

25. 105y - 96
26. 16k + 31
27. -21k
28. -14x + 13

29. 10z
30. 22k + 6
31. 42k + 39
32. 5m - 23

33. 7k + 16
34. -11z - 6
35. -11z
36. 4x + 39

37. -7x + 18
38. 14k + 11
39. 28m - 28
40. -2y + 19

41. 27x + 10
42. -17x - 5
43. 34k + 34
44. -20y - 10

45. -29x + 30
46. -29k - 5
47. -9
48. -3x

49. 7z + 2
50. -x + 3
51. -9z - 25
52. 8z - 20

53. 15x
54. 260y + 389
55. 17z - 10
56. 19z + 13

57. 9x + 9
58. -19k
59. -10y - 11
60. -13m + 4

61. 48x - 86
62. 6x
63. -6m
64. 5x

65. -27y + 33
66. -132m + 214
67. 8y + 15
68. 11x

69. 12
70. -6z
71. -10y
72. 30k + 10

73. -19y
74. -24x + 5
75. -2k - 13
76. 2k + 2

77. 11x - 12
78. -2m + 13
79. -15z
80. 19y - 5

81. -16y + 20   82. -18y   83. -7x + 6   84. 2m + 24

85. 12k   86. 33m   87. -20z + 14   88. -8m - 21

89. -16k + 8   90. 44z - 26   91. 27k + 26   92. -21m - 18

93. 35x + 36   94. -18z + 8   95. -11k + 1   96. 36k + 50

97. 23m + 23   98. 16x + 15   99. -17k + 4   100. -19m + 32

101. -25x + 33   102. -21z + 8   103. y + 6   104. -11k + 17

Page 43: Evaluating Equations

1. 48   2. 10   3. -50   4. 16   5. 384   6. 5   7. -30   8. 6

Page 44: Evaluating Equations

1. -44   2. -19   3. 2   4. 22   5. 37   6. -35   7. 10   8. -11

Page 45: Evaluating Equations

1. 5   2. -49   3. -44   4. 1,260   5. 0   6. 50   7. -35

8. -4

Page 46: Evaluating Equations

1. -21   2. -24   3. -12   4. 12   5. 4   6. 18   7. 23   8. -9

Page 47: Evaluating Equations

1. -1   2. -12   3. 9   4. 0   5. -1   6. 5   7. -3   8. 8

Page 48: Evaluating Equations

1. -27   2. -12   3. 8   4. 69   5. 4   6. -31   7. -41   8. -42

Page 49: Evaluating Equations

1. -54   2. 8   3. 13   4. -12   5. -7   6. 6   7. -9   8. -27

Page 50: Evaluating Equations
1. -3   2. -34   3. -19   4. 6   5. 23   6. -69   7. 0   8. -36

Page 51: Evaluating Equations
1. 9   2. -54   3. -10   4. -38   5. 77   6. 46   7. -3   8. -3

Page 52: Evaluating Equations
1. -1   2. 57   3. 22   4. -29   5. 25   6. -8   7. 4   8. 22

Page 53: Standard Linear Equations

1. 2	11. 3	21. 9
2. -9	12. 8	22. -6
3. 10	13. -8	23. -1
4. 8	14. 10	24. 0
5. 7	15. -10	25. 10
6. 4	16. -10	26. 7
7. 7	17. -2	27. 4
8. -10	18. -7	28. -7
9. 5	19. -6	29. -8
10. 10	20. 8	30. -7

1. (-1, 11)
2. (2, -3.167)
3. (1.915, -1.915)
4. (1.652, -1.452)
5. No real solution.
6. (0.828, -1.328)
7. (-1, 5)
8. (2.582, -2.582)
9. (-0.348, 1.148)
10. (1.612, -1.612)
11. (5.212, 0.288)
12. (3, -3)
13. (10, -5)
14. (2.5, 1)
15. (-4, 4.667)
16. (4.5, -7.5)
17. (-1.07, 1.87)
18. (7, -7)
19. No real solution.
20. (-6.333, 3)
21. (-1.852, 1.852)
22. (12, -12)
23. (1.385, -9.385)
24. (1.054, -1.054)
25. (0.898, -3.898)
26. (1.14, -1.14)
27. (5, -5)
28. (-9, 4.5)
29. (1.2, -1)
30. (1.686, -1.186)
31. (4.5, -4.5)
32. (12.076, -1.076)
33. (-1.674, 5.674)
34. (1, -3.333)
35. (-1.333, -0.5)
36. (1, -0.25)
37. (-9, 5)
38. No real solution.
39. (2.5, -3.667)
40. (8.162, 1.838)

www.ingramcontent.com/pod-product-compliance
Lightning Source LLC
Chambersburg PA
CBHW080941120726
48003CB00011B/3242